A COLORING BOOK

I Love Insects

Coloring Book

Jose Valladares

This edition published in 2021 by Circlesquare Projections

ISBN: 978-1-7369559-7-0

Circlesquare Projections Publishing Company Pacoima, CA, 91331

Table of Contents

Introduction

Insects consist of three part body, three pair of legs, and one pair of antennae. These little creatures represent more than half of all living things.
I love insects coloring book is a good way to know the names of these smazing little creatures.
It is easy to color these beautiful insects; helps you learn their names, and improves your creativity.

You will find 50 beautiful illustrations. One design per page to prevent colors to bleed through.

You will need the following supplies:

- Crayola pencils or prism color colored pencils premier

- Blending pencils - helps you blend colors together

- Pencil sharpener

- Brush tip markers

- A storage container for storing all your supplies

It is easy and fun to color these insects designs and I hope you enjoy coloring these pages.

Have fun!

2

Butterfly

3

Ladybug

Scarab beetle

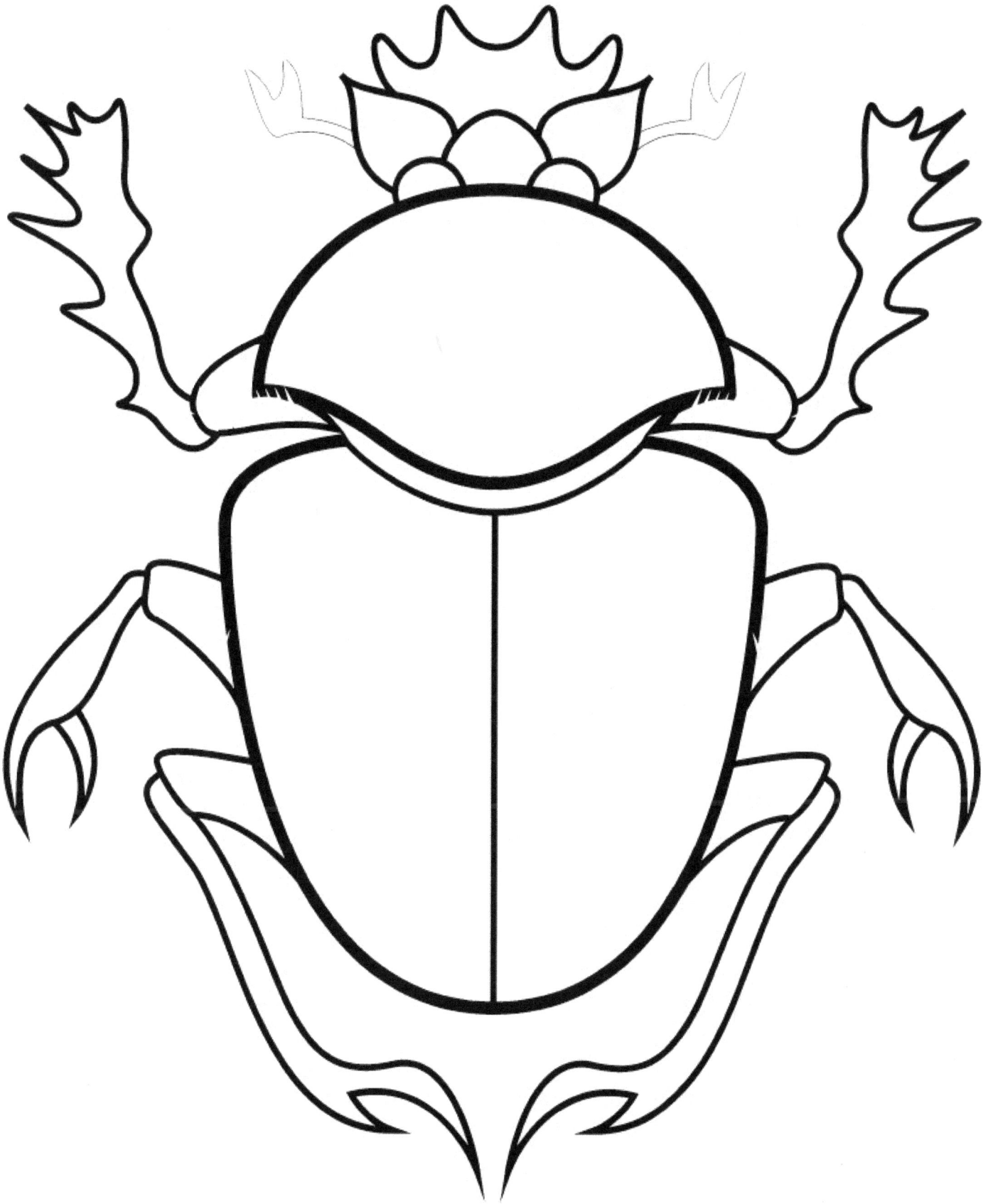

Morning light

Brown marmorated stink bug

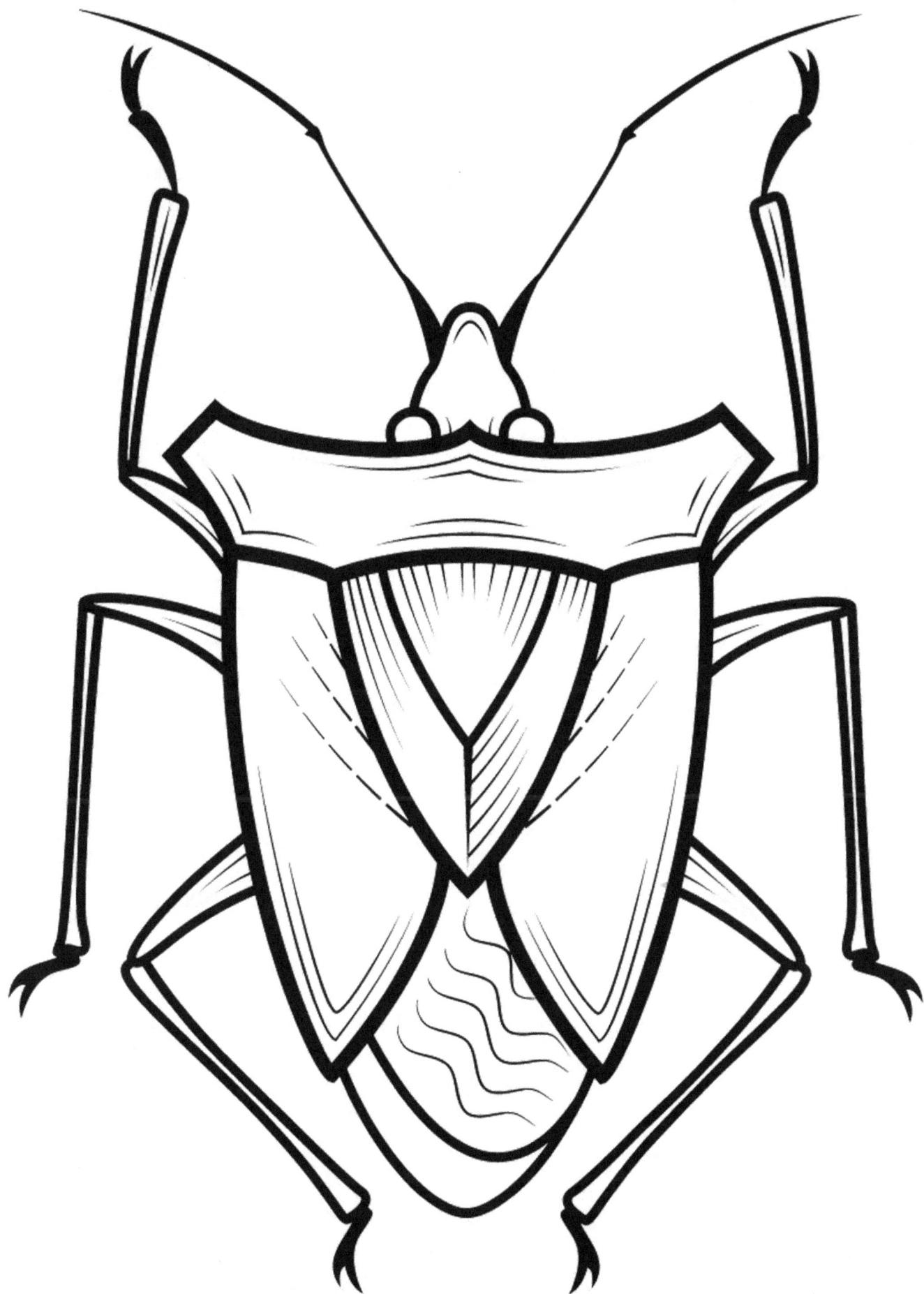

Colorful butterfly

Peaceful morning

Moth

Leaf insect

19

Centipede

Cricket

Cockroach

Ant

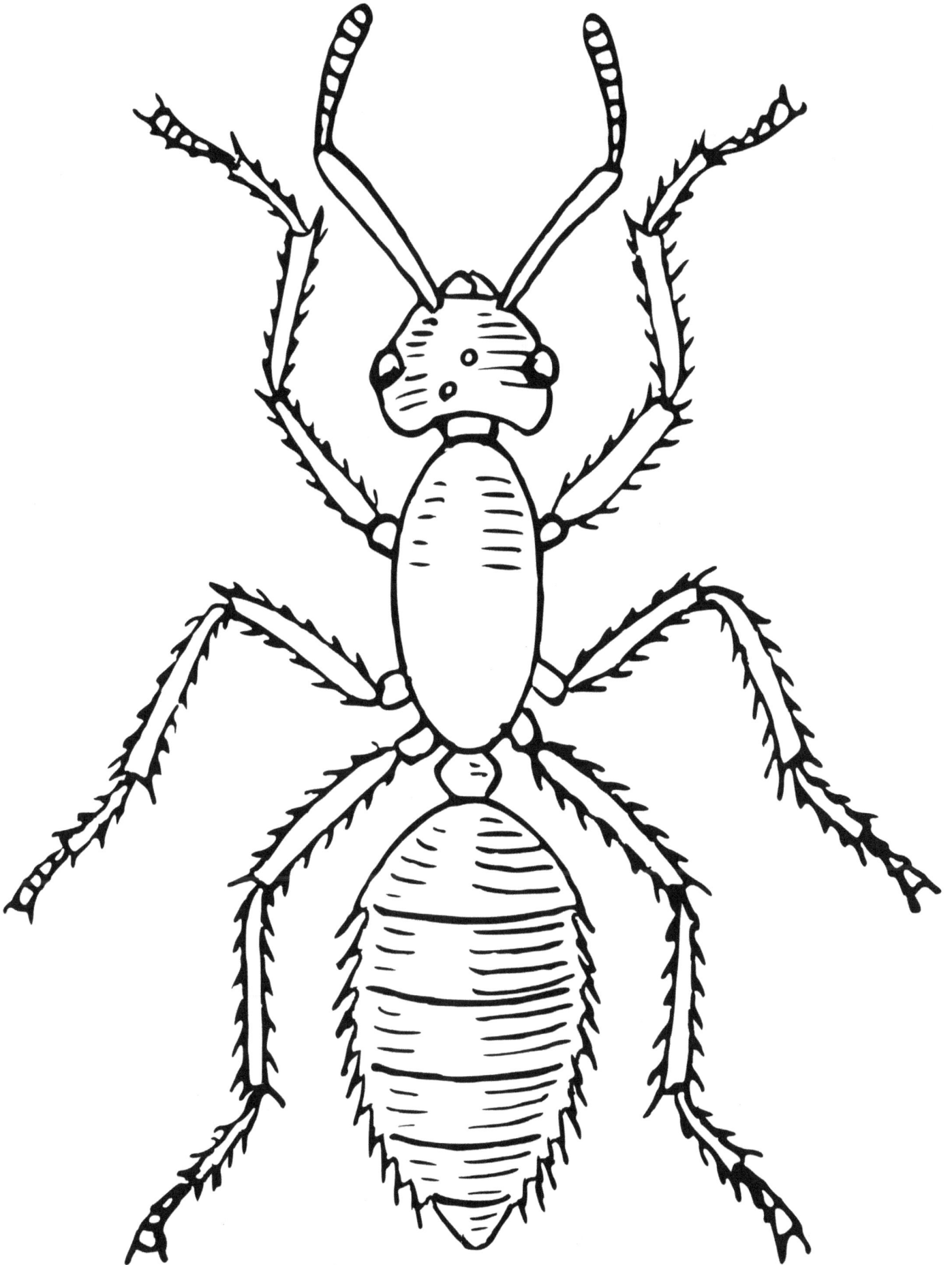

Black widow spider

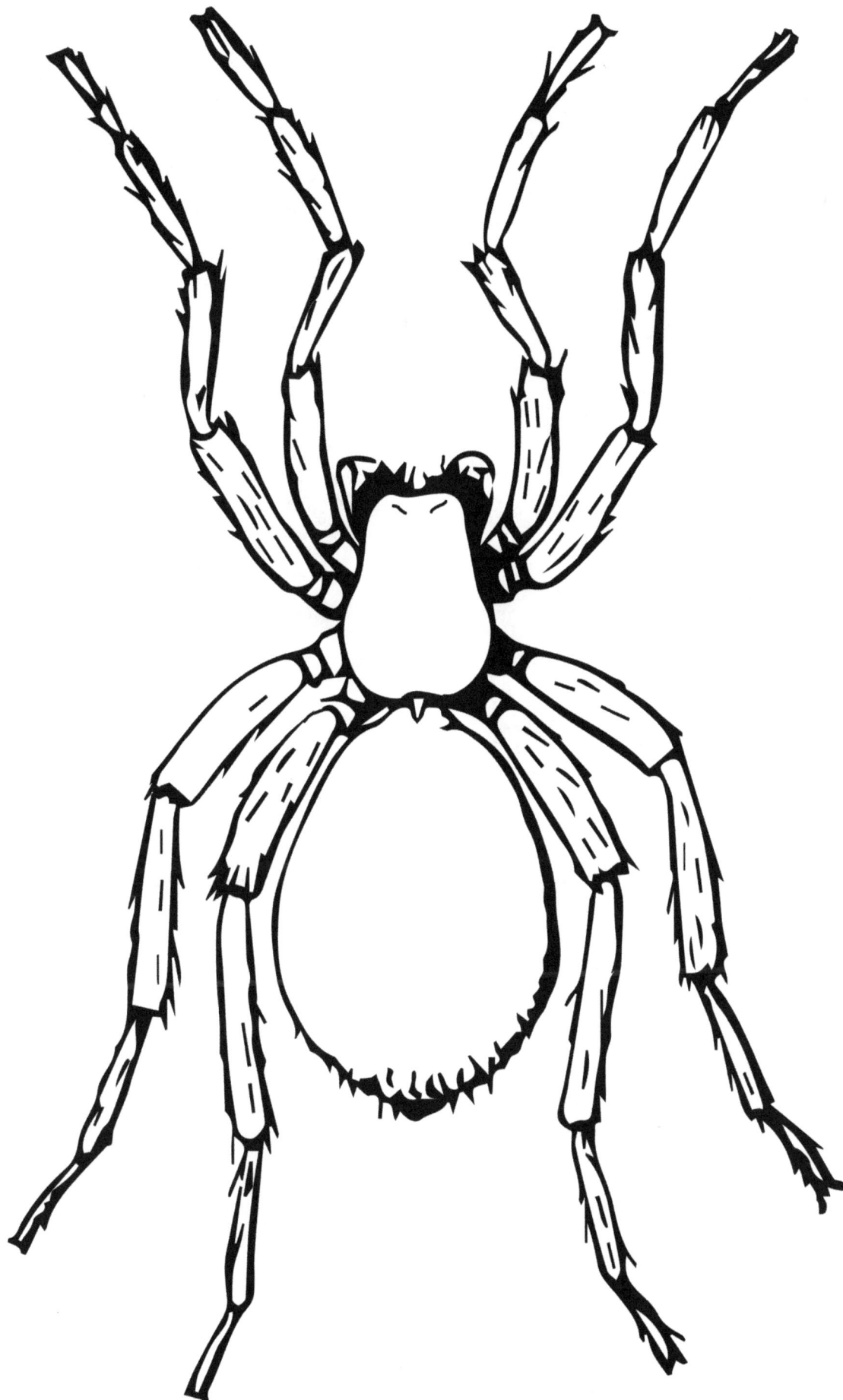

31

I love insects

33

Grasshopper

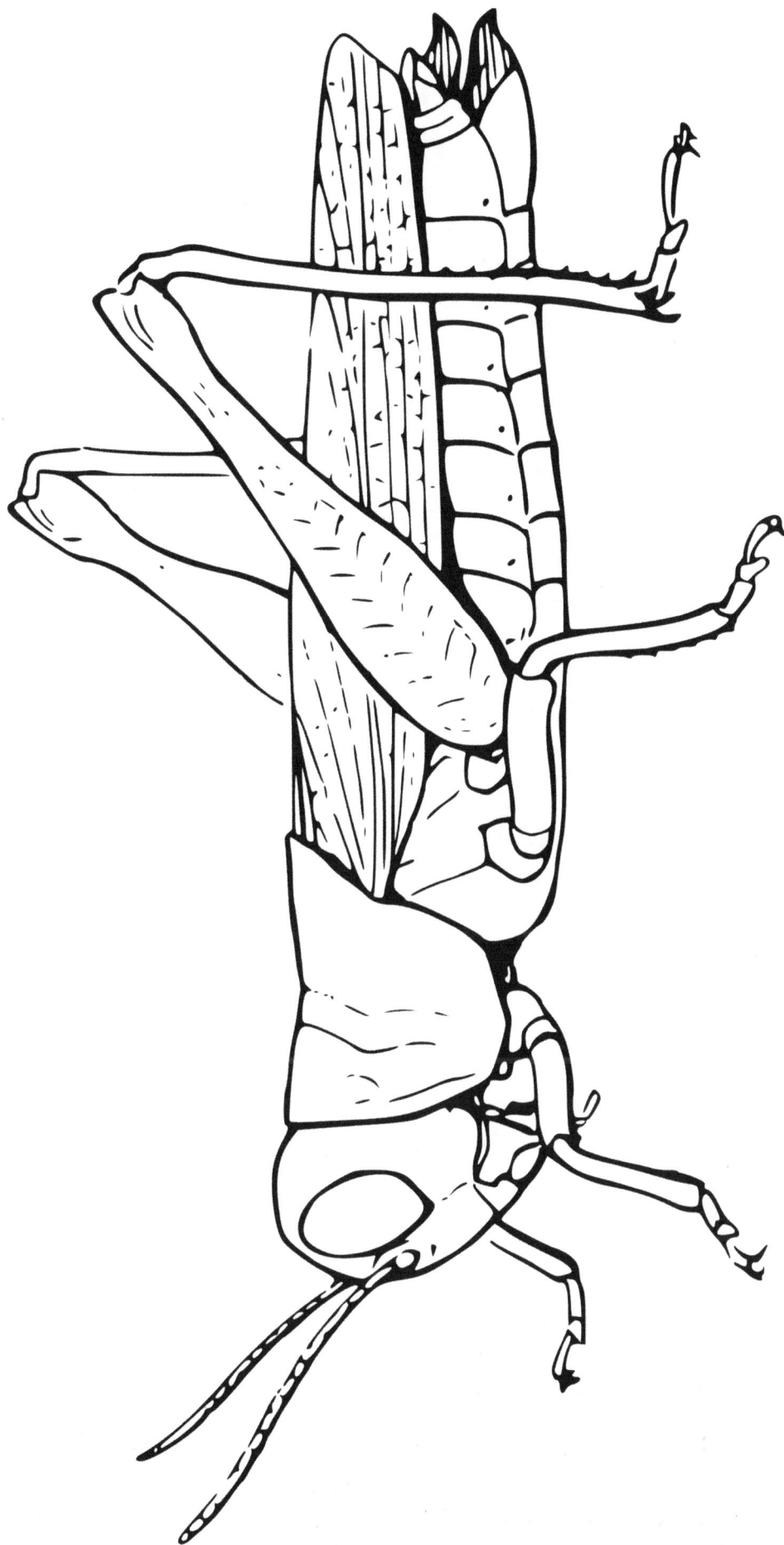

Scorpion

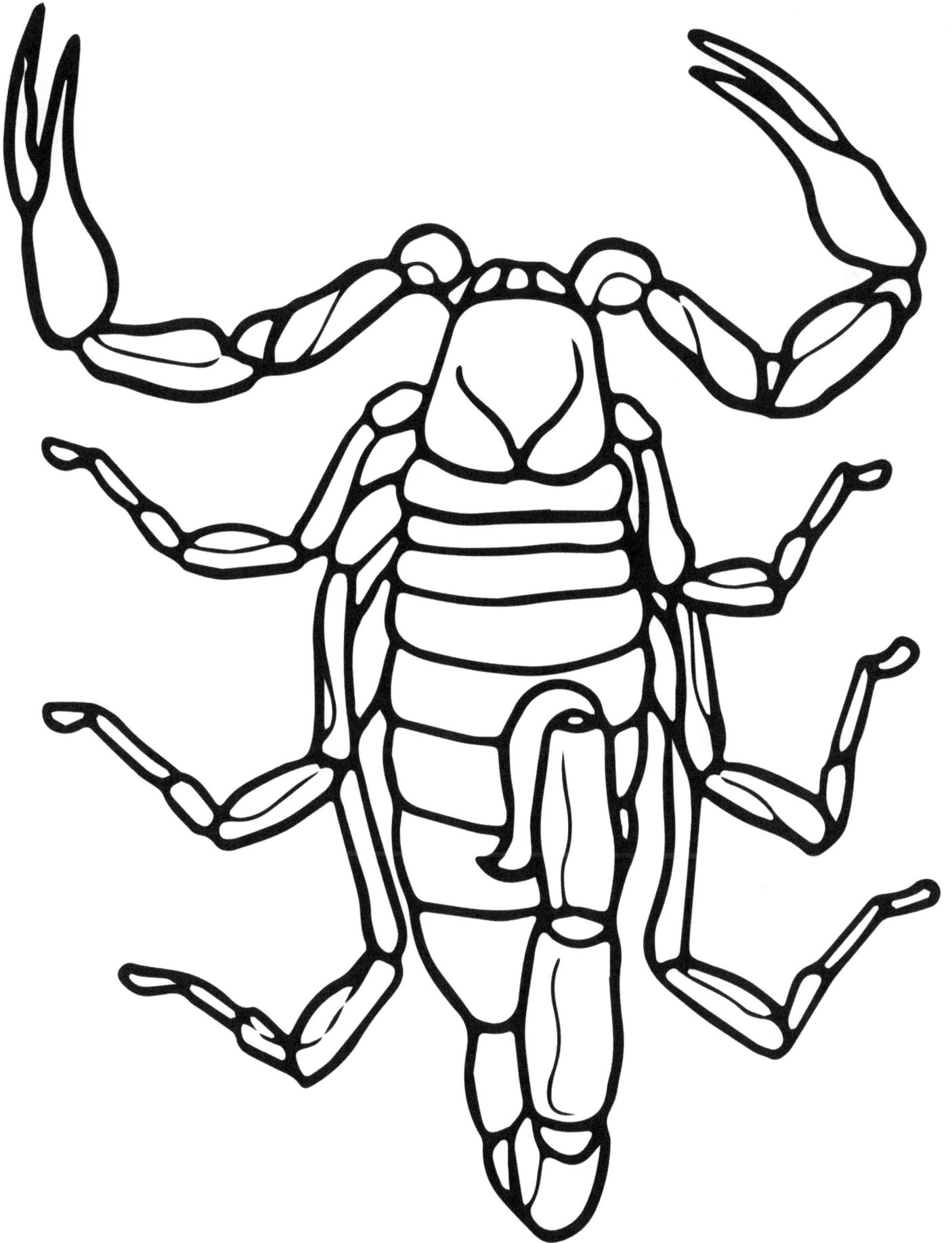

37

Odontolabis mouhotii elegans beetle

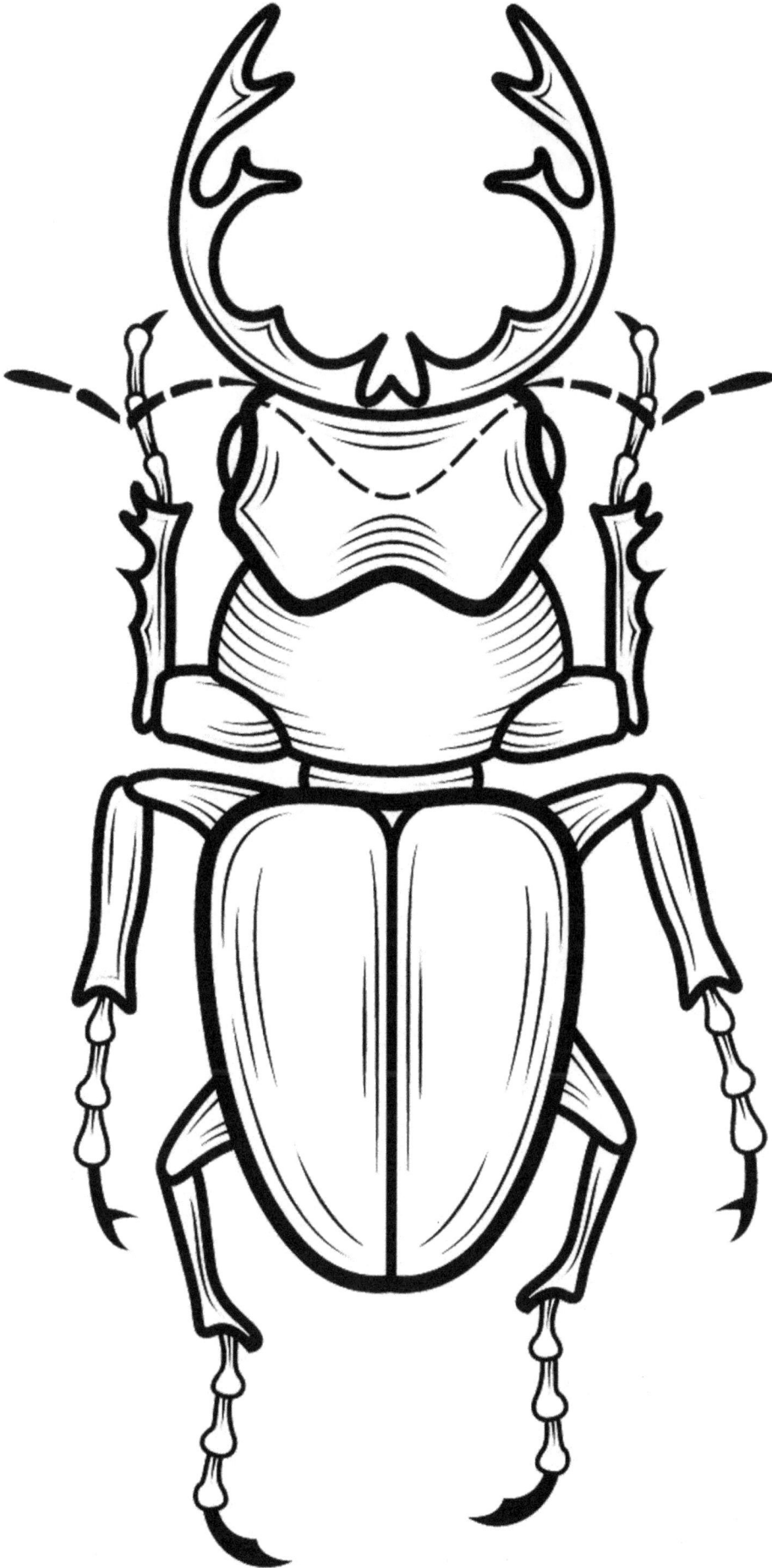

Fly

41

Dragonfly

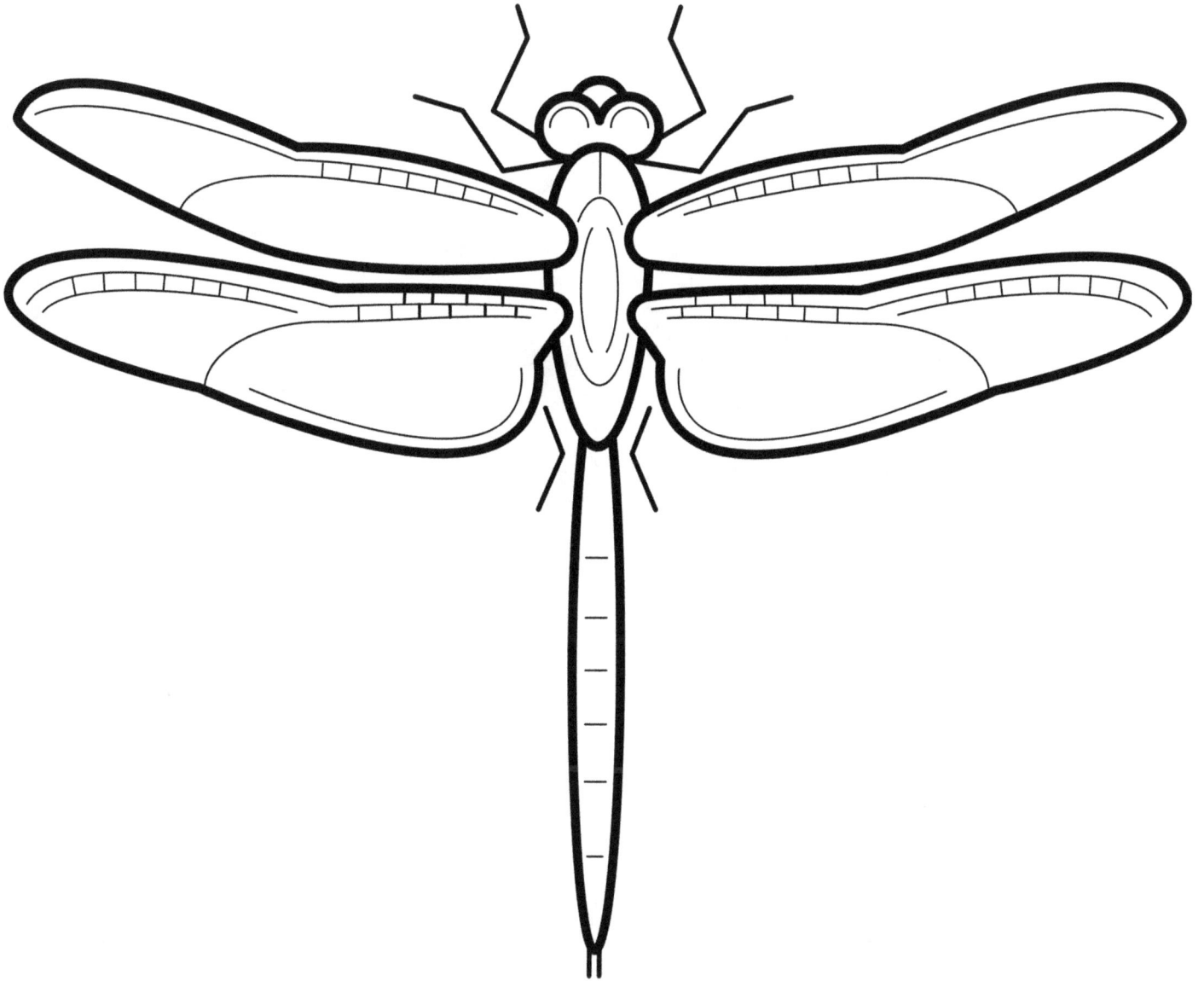

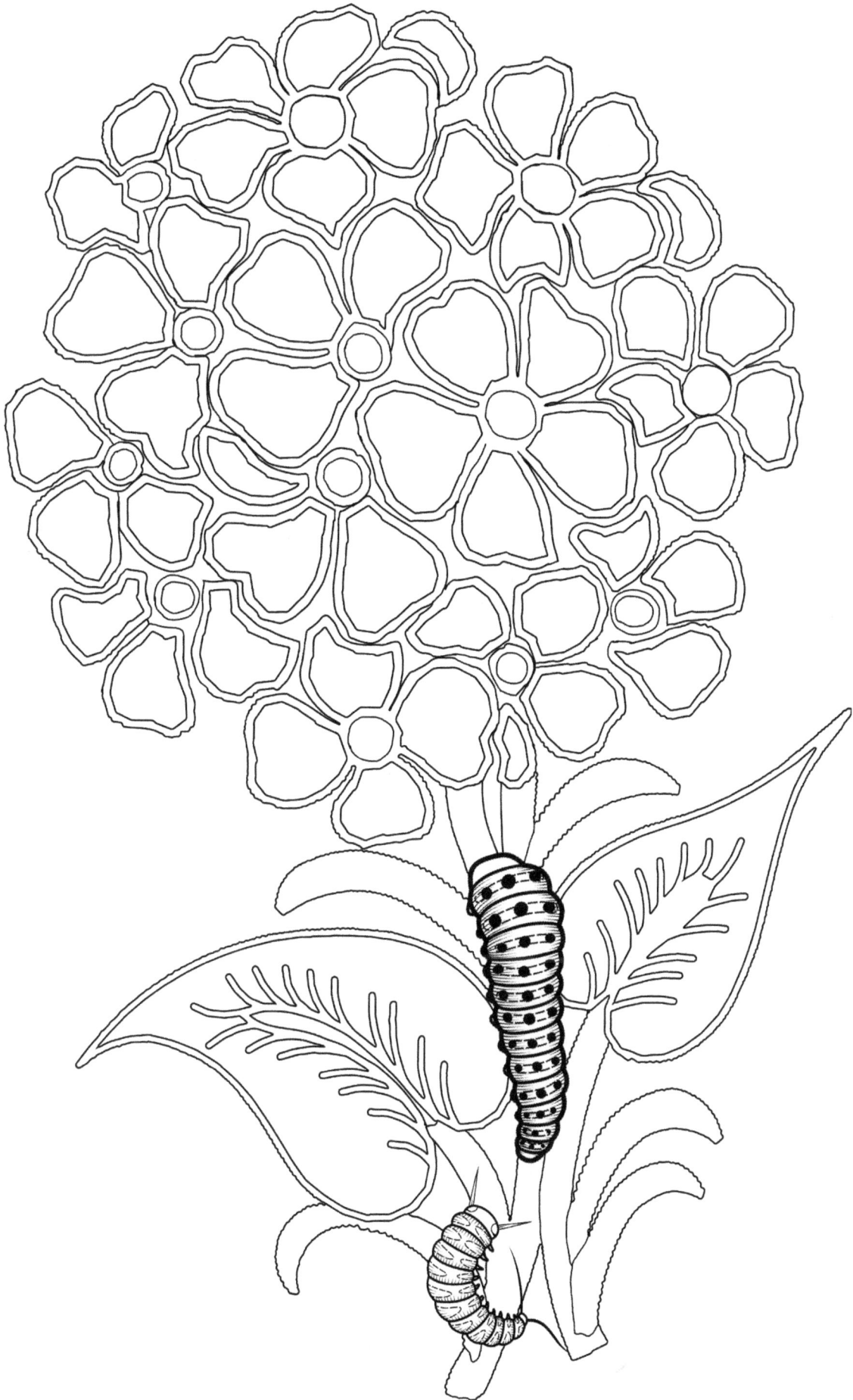

Summer

47

Palo verde beetle

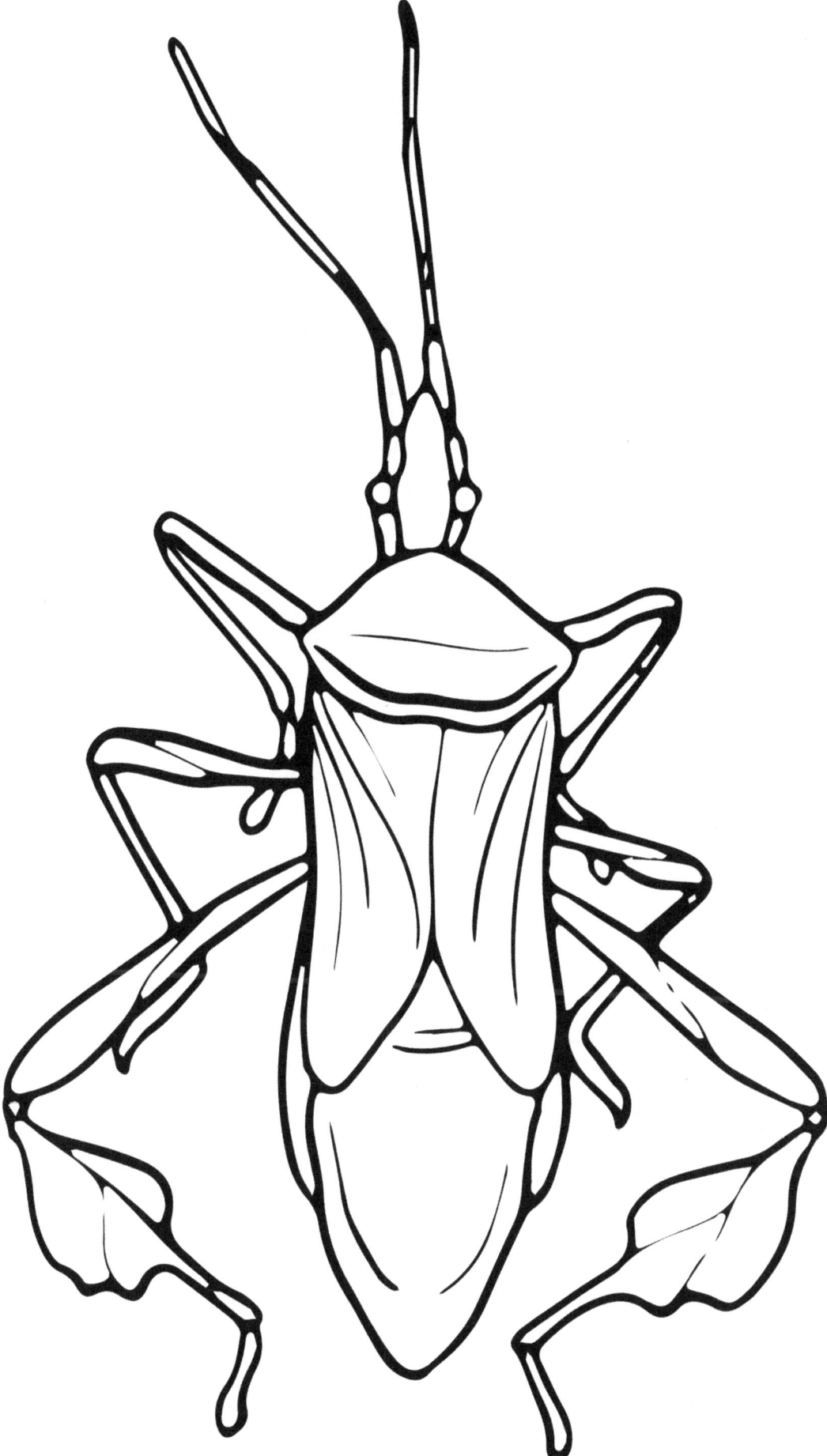

49

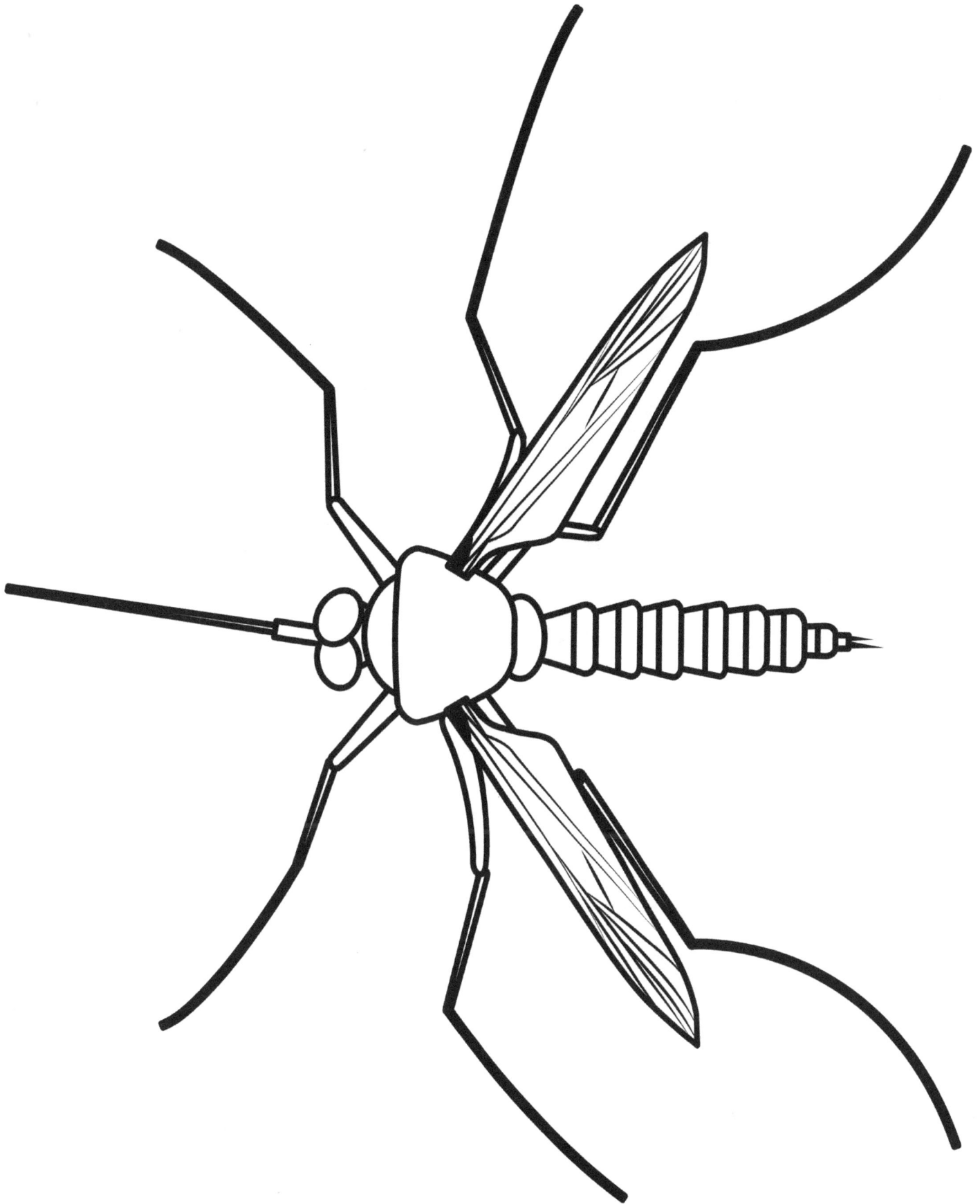

Mosquito

51

longhorn wooden bug

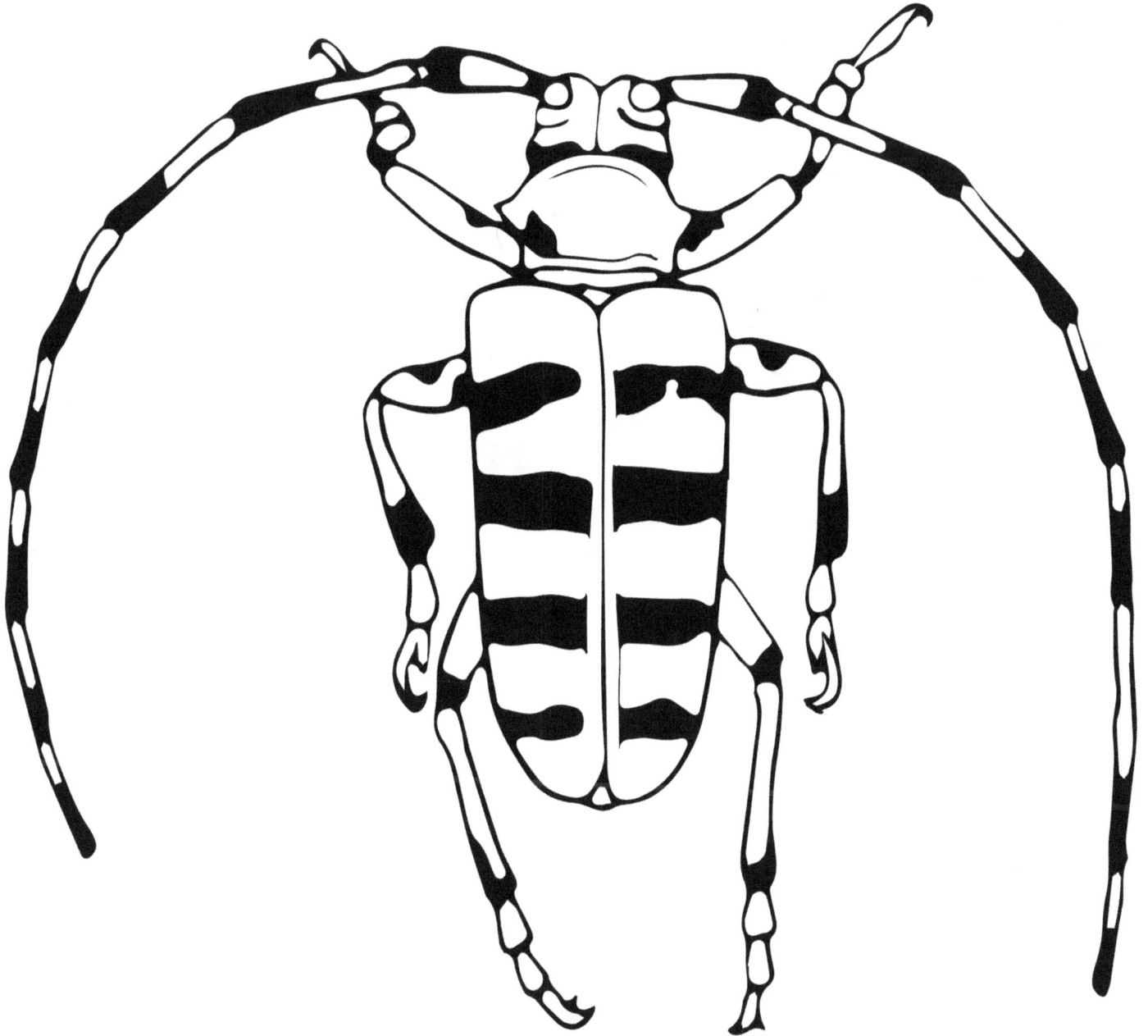

Skimmer

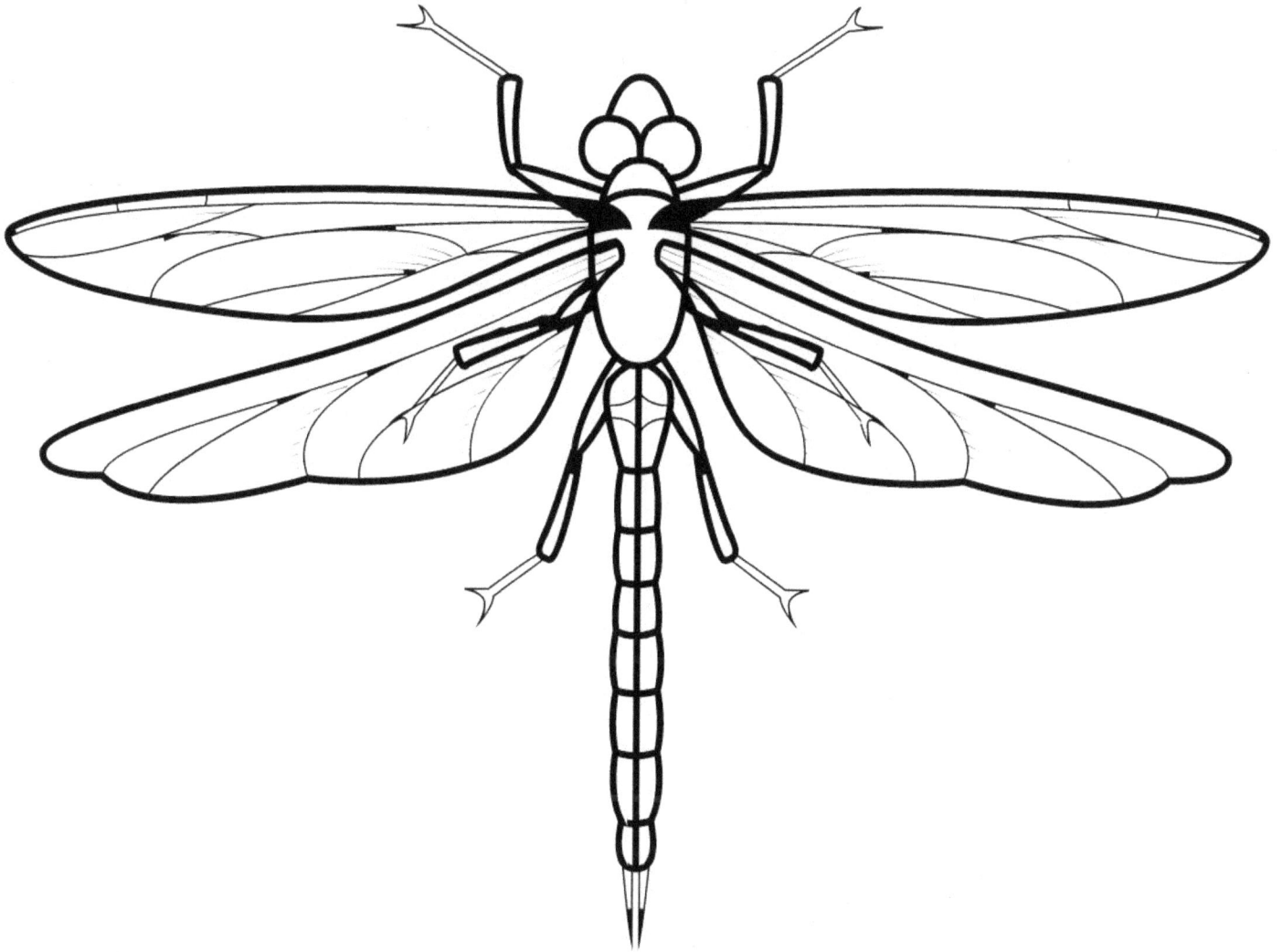

Fall

57

Silkmoth

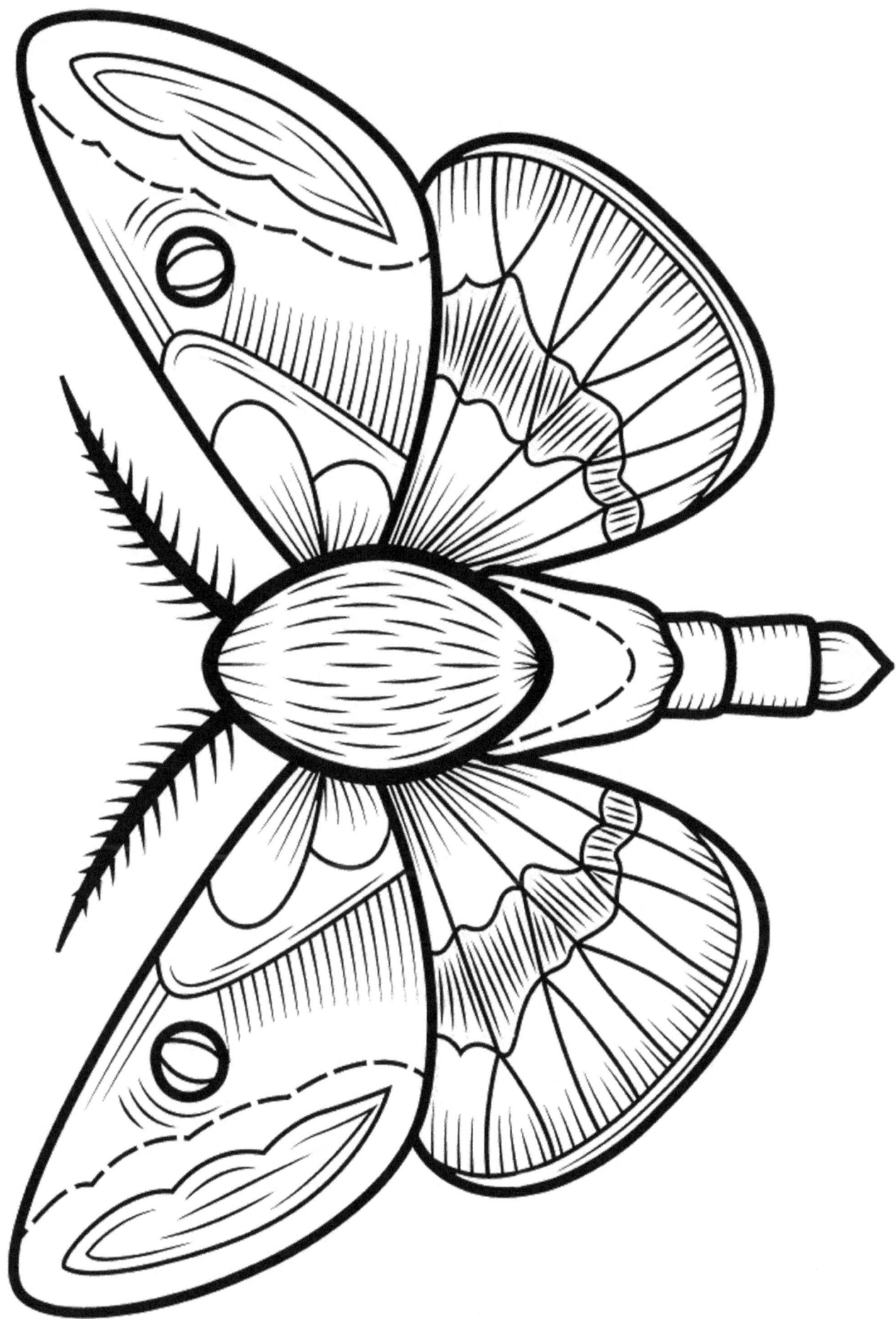

Worm

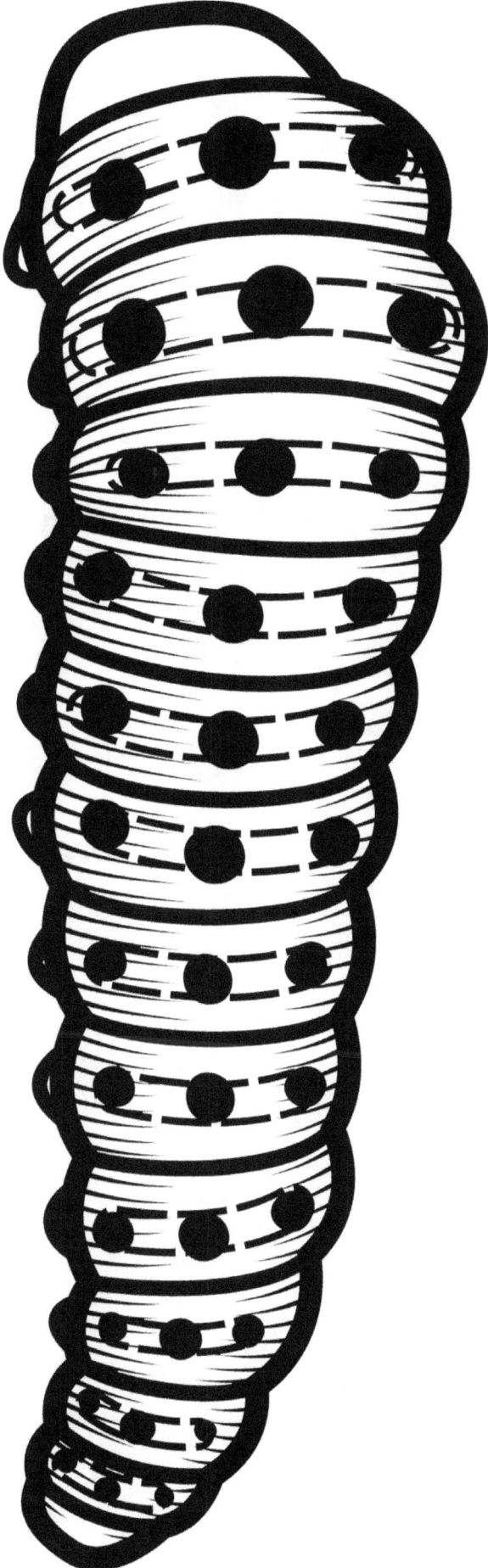

Chrysina gloriosa beetle

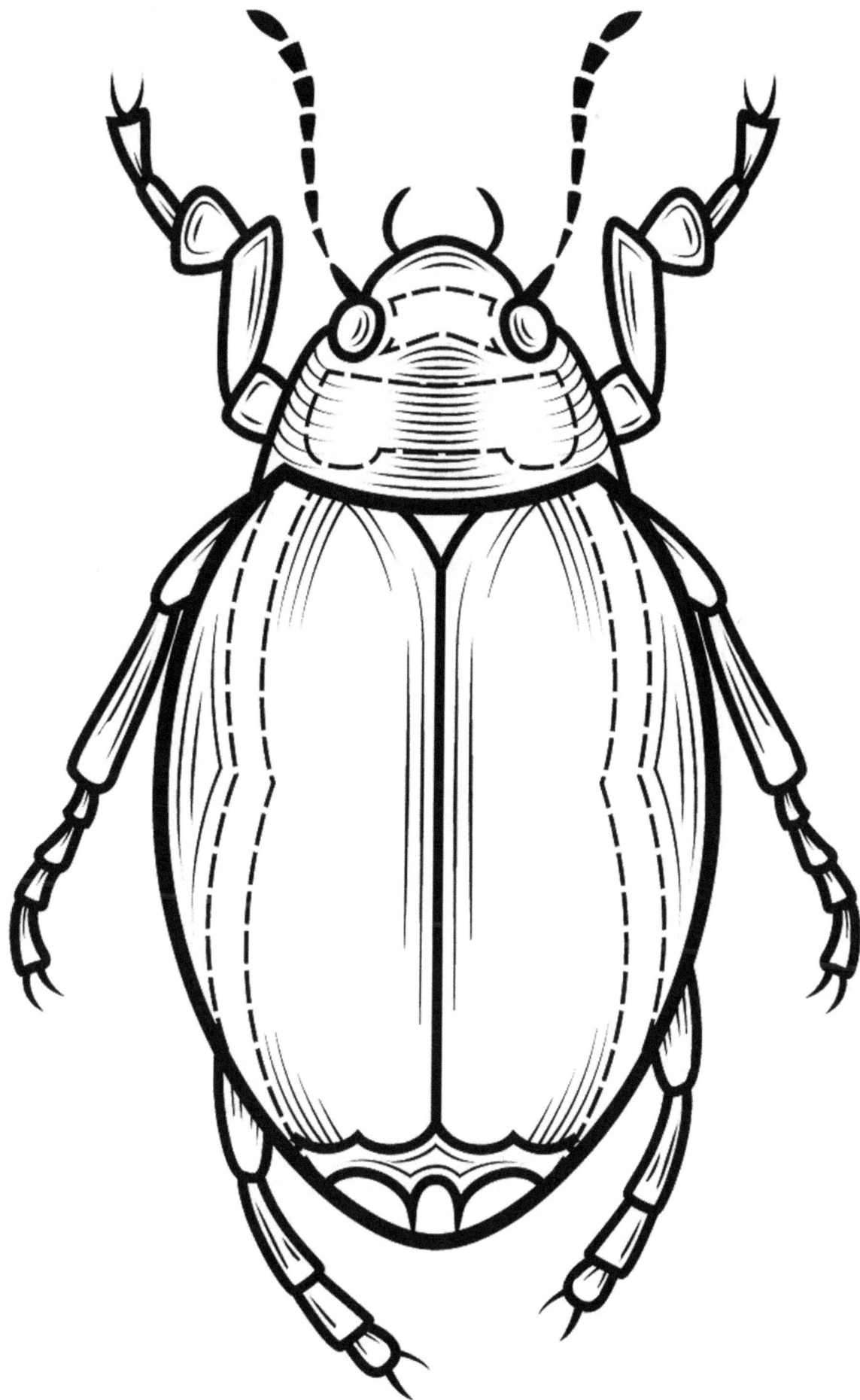

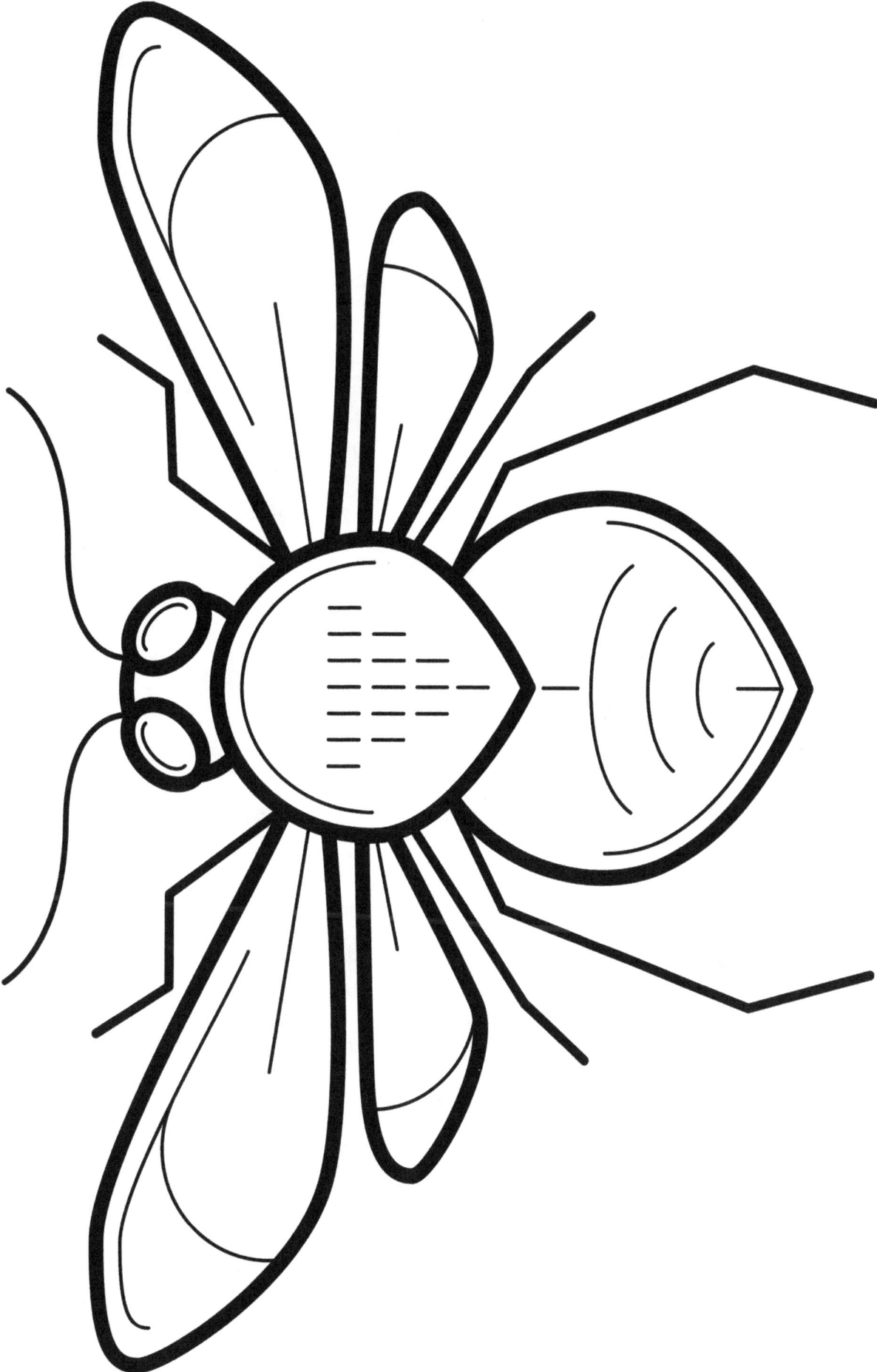

Flying bee

Bedbug

Worm

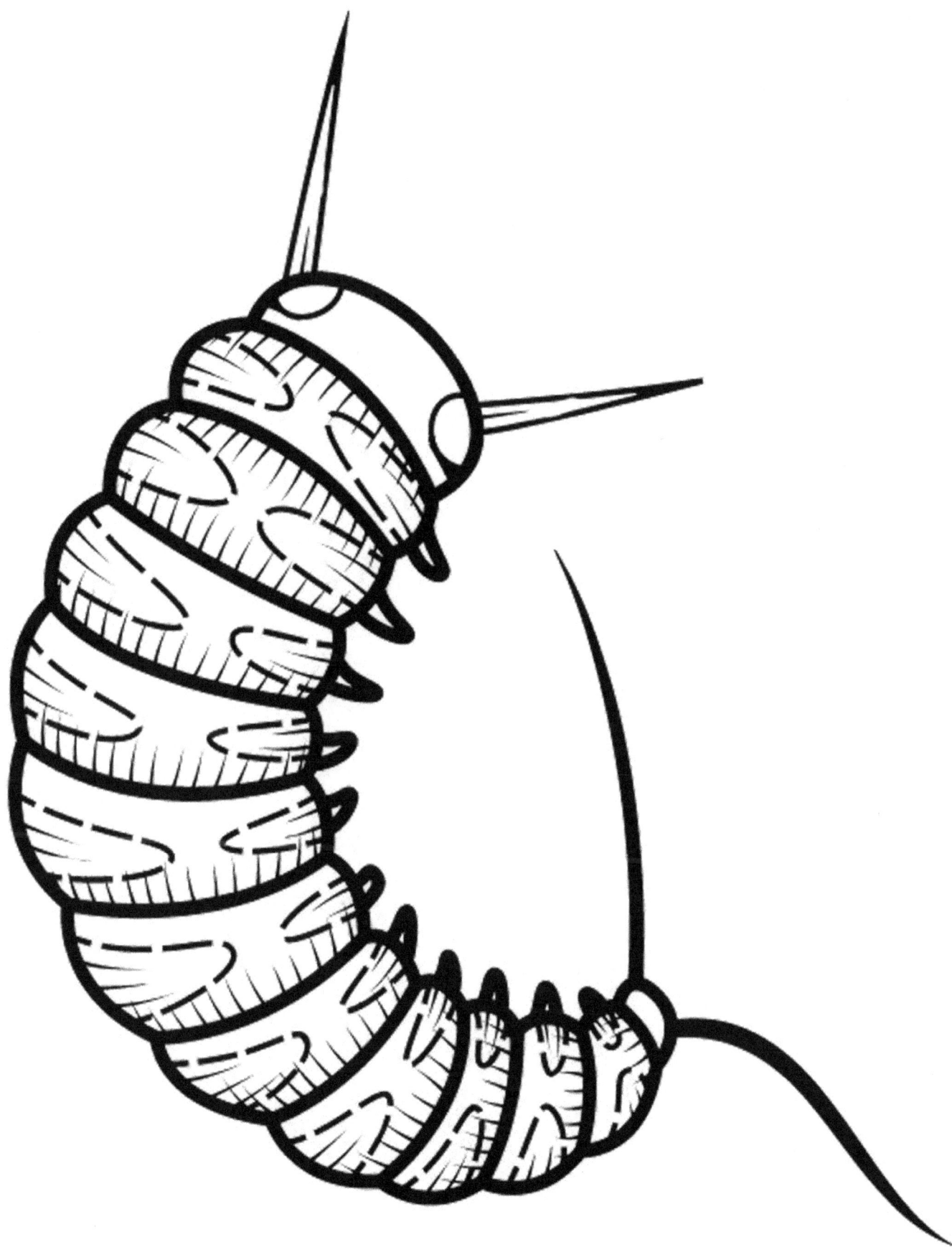

American fly

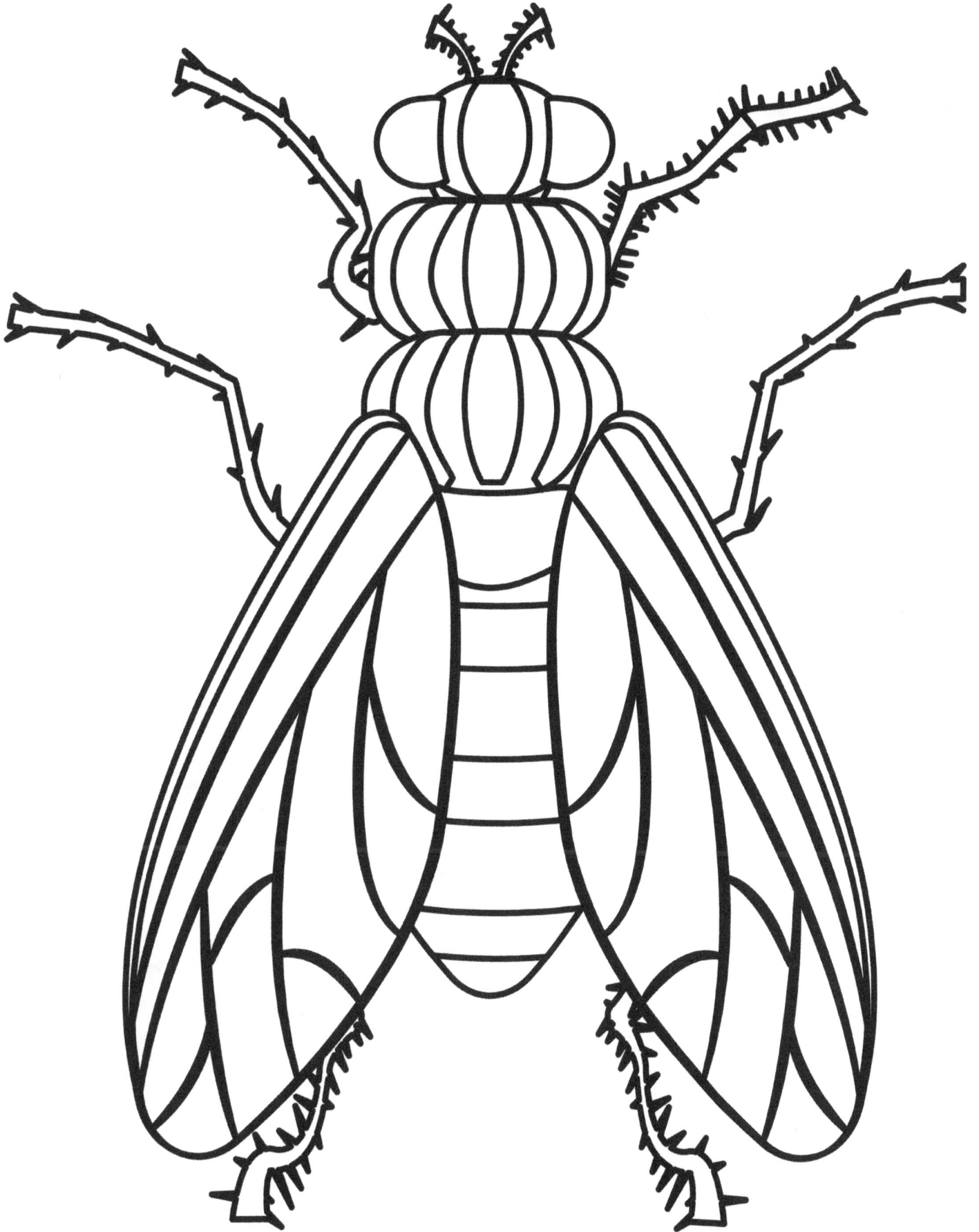

Xylotrupes gideon beetle

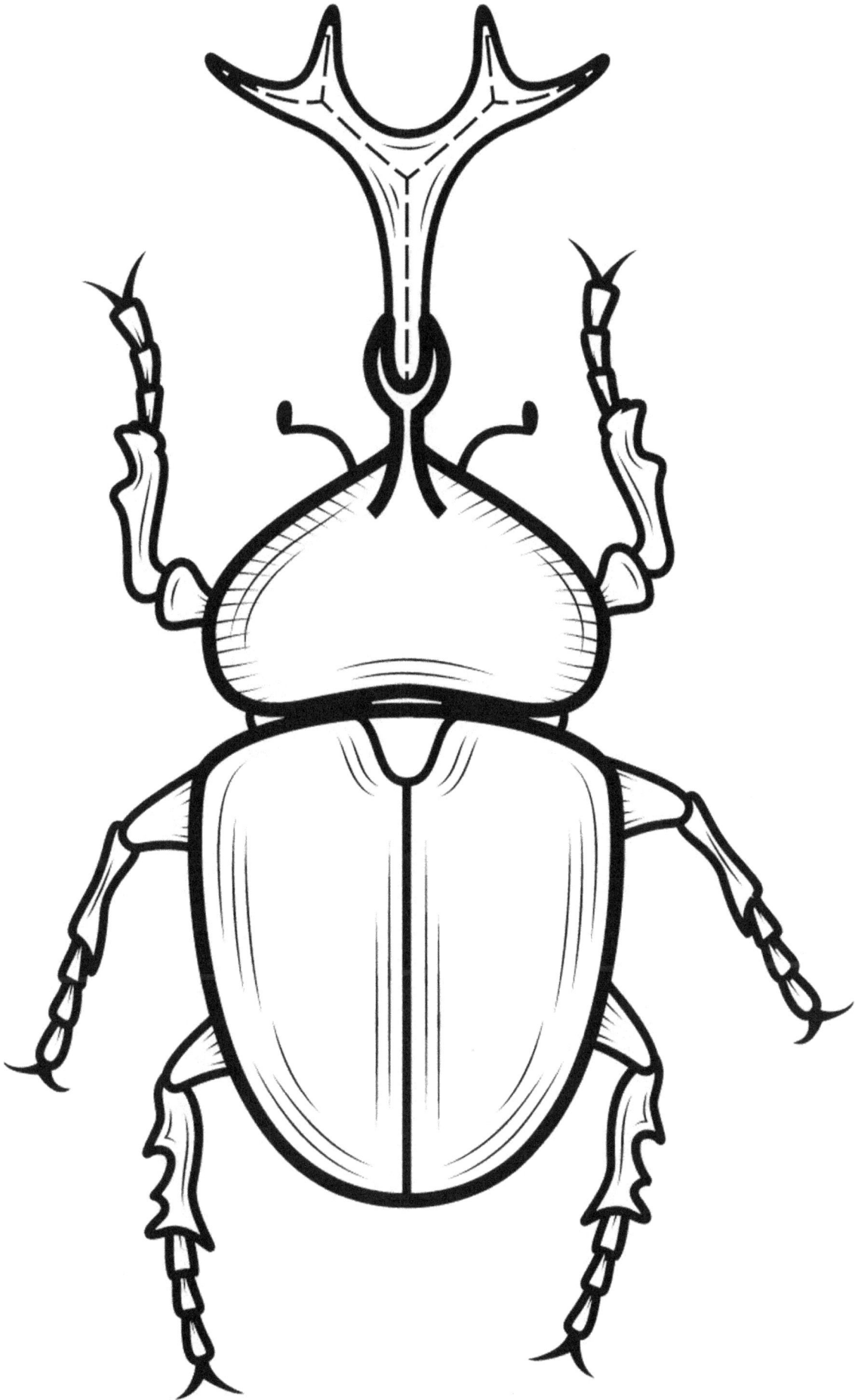

acherontia lachesis moth

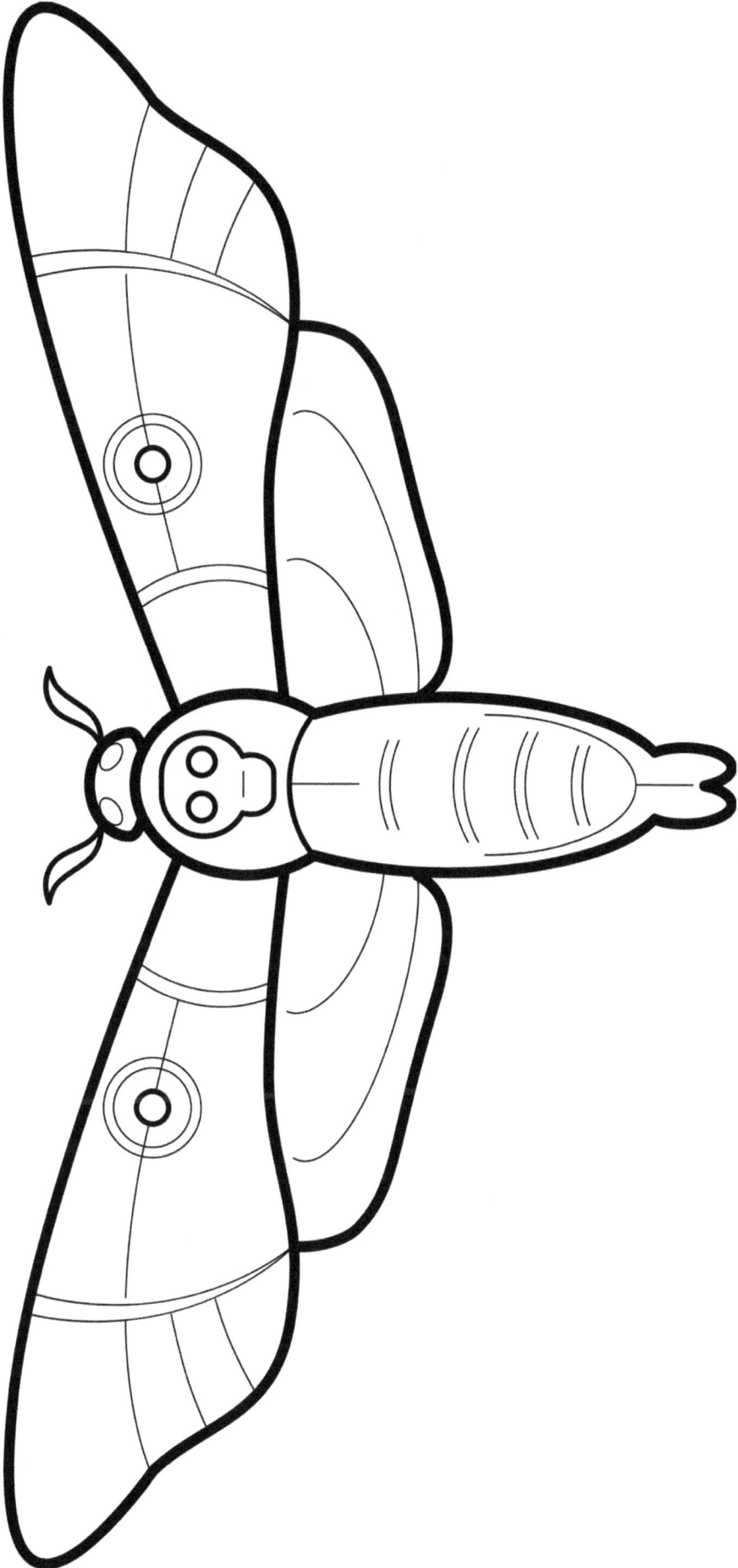

79

Honey bee

Peace & love

83

Stenochidus cyanescens beetle

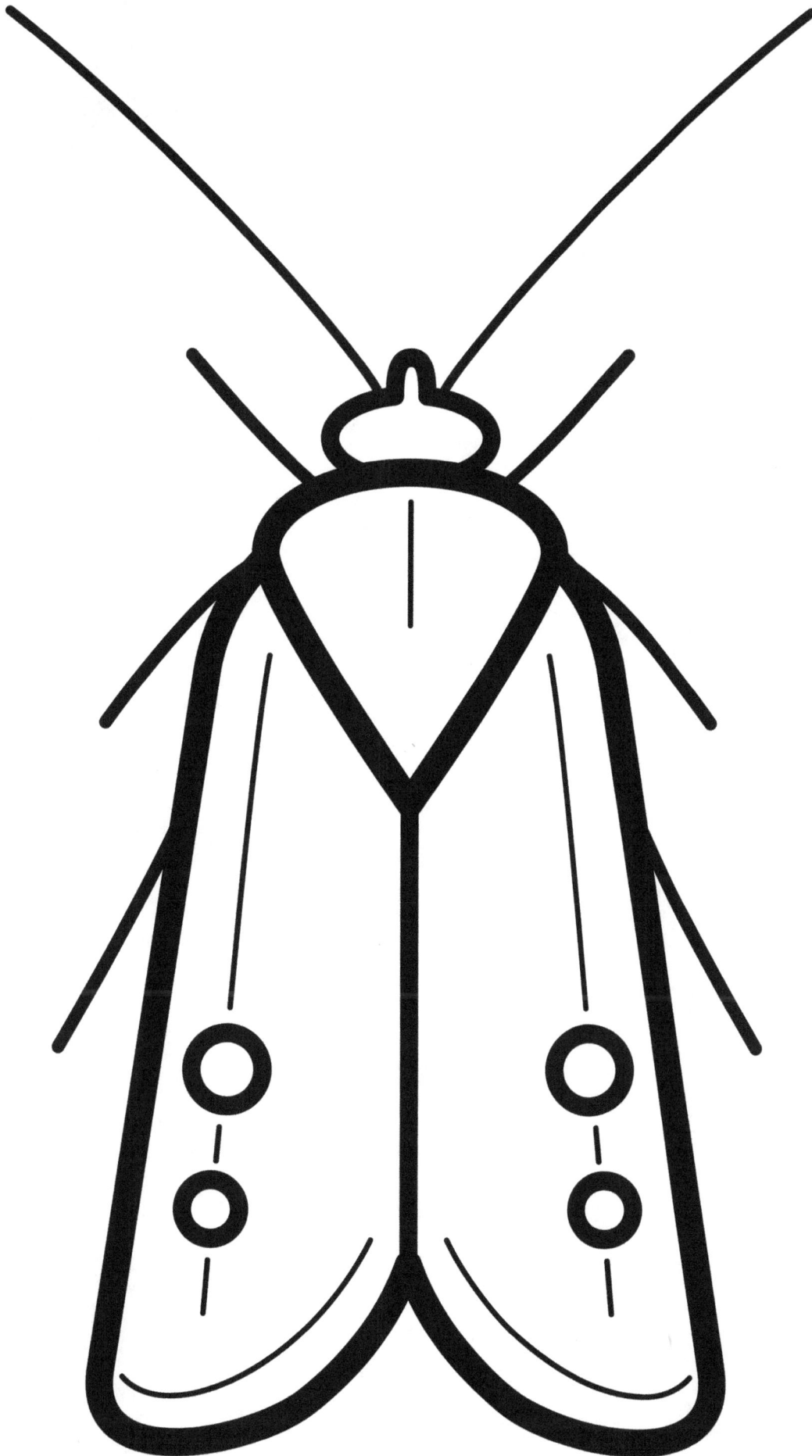

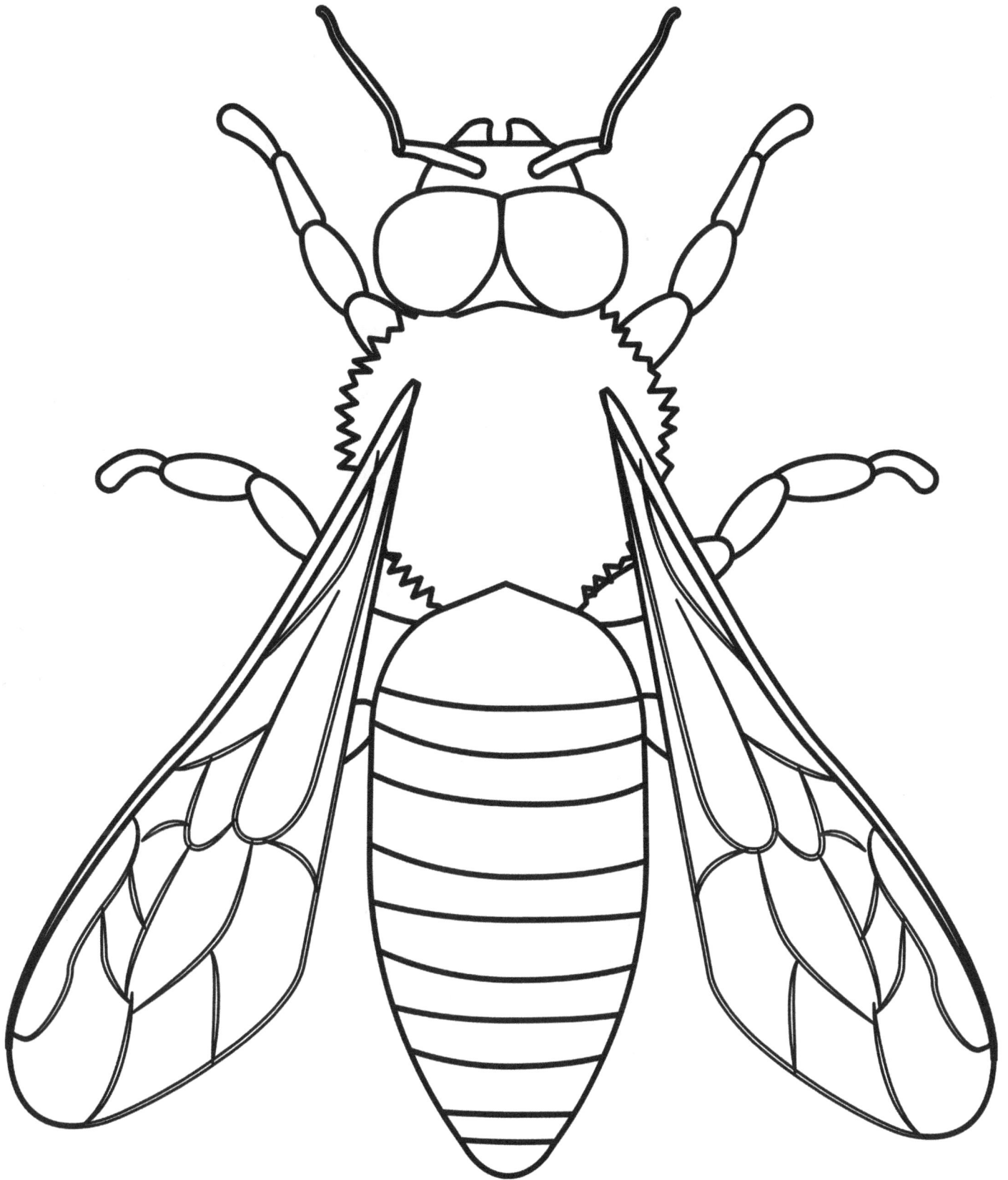

Wasp

87

Crum

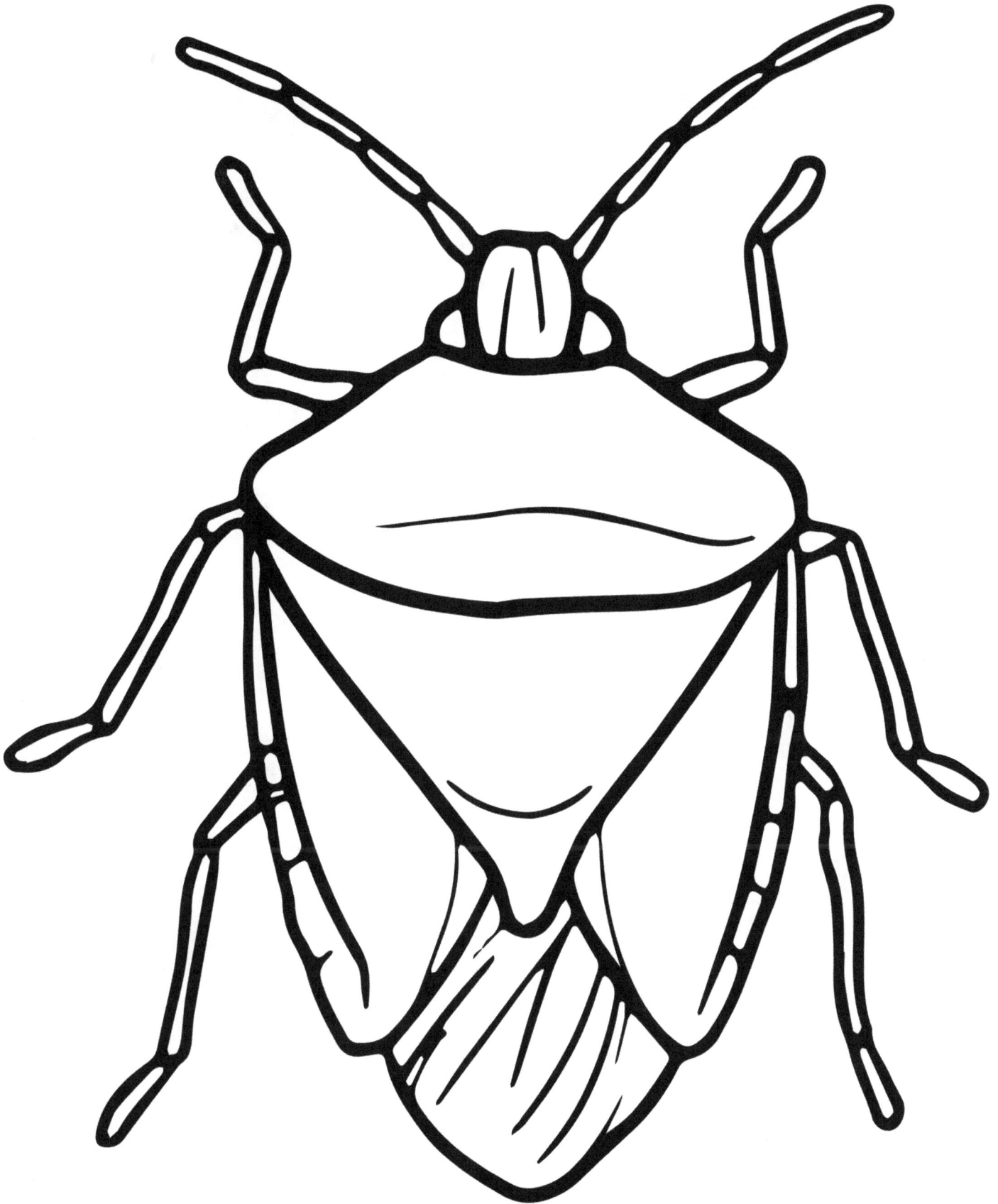

Sunset

Silkmoth

93

Eclipse

95

Good times

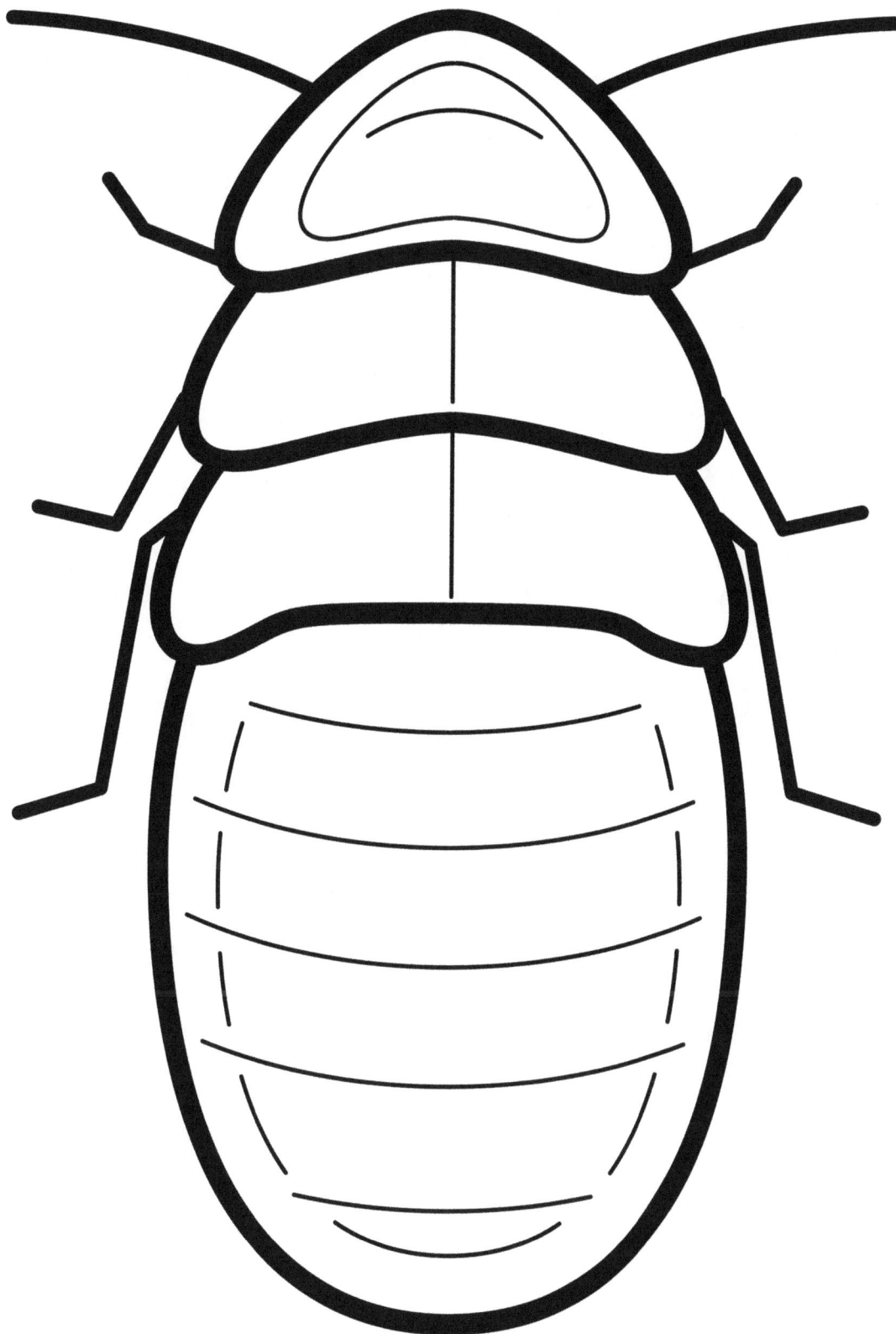

Baby roach

Butterfly

Acknowledgements

Some images and designs were use with permission from freepik.com

Some images and designs were use with permission from pexels.com

Some images and designs were use with permission from vexels.com

Some images and designs were use with permission from pixabay.com

Some images and designs were use with permission from depositphotos.com

Designed by macrovector / freepik following pages;
5,7,11, 13, 17, 39, 55, 59, 61, 63, 71, 77, 81, 93, 101

Cover disigned by brgfx / freepik

www.ingramcontent.com/pod-product-compliance
Lightning Source LLC
Chambersburg PA
CBHW081648270326
41933CB00018B/3392